Explorations of a Cosmic Soul

This book is the physical manifestation of lessons learned through the school of everyday life.
It is for the seeker. The one who chooses to dive into unexplored depths. It is for the one who is ready to meet the truth within themselves.
It is for you.
May you connect to the universe inside.

Foreword

by Jill Wintersteen of Spirit Daughter
(Astrologist, and overall magical human)

In the current transformative time both cosmically and earthly, we have been given a few shining stars- beacons of light to guide us on our journey. Allie Michelle is one of them. Her poetry and the energy it imbues provides a pathway from dark to light, from untruth to truth and from destruction to nourishment. A path that parallels the movement of our stars and the story of the universe.

In the past six months, there has been a steady shift in energy in the collective consciousness, a changing of the guards so to speak, and with that, we are witnessing the rise of the feminine energy. Feminine energy by this definition is one that heals, one that nourishes, one that is of service and one that is powerful enough to give life to any area that needs it.

It has long been predicted by shamans, yoga masters, and spiritual teachers that women will heal this planet with their feminine energy. They will heal the Earth from the destruction of war, they will heal society from its ego-driven insecurities, and they will heal our relationships with each other. What has been a long-standing prediction is now evidenced by the movement of the stars, and the movement of the feminine voice.

In 2011, a star known as Regulus transitioned from Leo to Virgo. Regulus holds the energy of regality, leadership, and defense of these positions. For over 2000 years Regulus was home to the lion constellation that formed his very heart. And over the last 600 years, Regulus was in the last third of Leo which is ruled by Mars, the planet of war. No wonder so much blood has been shed and whole societies were left heartbroken during this time. Where Leo represents masculine leadership, Virgo represents an empowered woman, self-sufficient and capable of great healing.

Regulus has shifted into the first part of Virgo ruled by Mercury, the planet of communication, and this energy is influencing the way both male and female leaders communicate with each other and their community. With Regulus entering Virgo, this kingly star is shifting from King to Queen and God to Goddess.

Kings rule by power, Queens rule through service. They both have power, they both are rulers, leaders, and teachers but their approach is very different. In August of 2017, we experienced an amazing Total Solar Eclipse in the Northern Hemisphere, particularly in North America, who has been a leader in the feminine movement since the sixties. This Eclipse took place within two degrees of Regulus providing an energetic catalyst to the shifting energy from Leo to Virgo. The Eclipse also occurred at the North Node in Leo, which gave the transiting energy a pathway.

North Nodes tell us where we are going- they outline our karmic path both individually and as a society. This combination of Regulus transitioning to Virgo combined with the North Node still giving us direction through Leo teaches us leadership based in service. It is the energy of individual kingdoms with the intent of serving humanity as their mission. This energy will usher in leaders with unity and compassion at the heart of their decisions and will bring forth a feminine perspective of healing for all.

The Solar Eclipse opened a portal for us to step through and on the other side, feminine energy is empowered, leading and healing our world. It's a process, though, and we've been witnessing it unfolding over the past few months. Feminine energy and the feminine voice has been suppressed for a long time and its rising is bound to bring about some friction, some shadow work and some drama.

When energy is subdued for a long period of time, its reemergence can be explosive. This emerging energy was given an extra push when Jupiter entered Scorpio in October of 2017, the same week the #MeToo movement started. Jupiter is the planet of expansion, while Scorpio is the underground, the shadow side and sign of hidden secrets.

When Jupiter met Scorpio's stars, combined with the already rising feminine, women all over joined as a community and expanded their voices and their hearts as they shared the hidden secrets within them. It was a necessary movement needed for the feminine to continue its awakening and its reclamation of power. The power that has always been hers to claim.

The rise of the feminine energy is preceded by the rise of the feminine voice, which will be fueled by a Lunar Eclipse in January and Solar eclipse in February. Both involve the energy of Aquarius, who is known for her outspokenness and ability to incite movement through her authentic voice.

At the time of this writing, these events have not occurred but it is this writer's prediction that there are many more movements on the horizon and women will become increasingly more outspoken about the fate of this planet. We will also see a rise in books like this one written by divine feminine leaders like Allie Michelle. They will inspire us and pass on heart-centered, healing messages through our communities.

In May, there will be another energetic charge for the feminine, and that is Uranus moving into Taurus. Uranus is the planet of change, forward movement and unknown shifts into new territory. He has been stationed in Aries for the last 8 years, which is a highly masculine sign. Aries is known as the God of war and the planet of the self. Taurus, on the other hand, is very feminine in nature. She is an Earth sign like Virgo, and known for her love of art and the Earth herself. She is the keeper of beauty and nature.

This transition from Aries to Taurus is much like the shifting of the star Regulus from Leo to Virgo. We are moving once again from self to community, from God to Goddess and from destruction to nourishment. All governed by the planet of change, Uranus. This transit will push the rise of the feminine into a new gear, one that will usher in permanent change and transformation. We will begin to see more focus on the collective instead of the self and we will lay down our ego-driven ways to help better the planet as a whole community.

Once again we will see the feminine energy developing steadily in each of us, men and women. A world ruled by feminine energy does not necessary mean a world ruled solely by women. The feminine will rise in each gender and men will learn to respect this part of themselves and let it guide them just like women have done for centuries.

So, what does a world dominated by feminine energy look like? When conflict arises, war will not be the only answer, new ways of negotiation will unfold. Nature herself will become more respected and made a priority in political agendas. There will be less ego involved in our countries decisions and service will become a priority. Women will become as powerful as men, and everyone will become equally respected no matter their ethnicities. New methods and paradigms will emerge in the way children are raised with both parents equally involved.

The stars are predicting not a role reversal per se, but a new way of doing things that has not been explored. It will be the true age of Aquarius- cutting edge, progressive and with the heart of humanity at its center. This is what a feminine future looks like. Most importantly women will remain feminine. They will keep and highlight their femininity, treasuring it as we treasure the energy of Virgo and Taurus. Their intuition will no longer be questioned and beaten down by logic. It, along will all their emotions, will be praised and used as guidance, not something to medicate or see as a burden. Women are different than men, their brains work differently, and that difference is what the world needs. This difference is what will restore balance and at the end of the day that is what's occurring - restoration of balance.

The following poetry is part of the restoration. It is feminine, it is born from intuition and emotion, it is beautiful. It inspires you to feel and reminds you that there is light in the world. The world may get a bit darker before we see the true emergence of light, but this book is a reminder that it is already here and balance is returning. Love, like you will read in this book, spreads like wildfire and won't take long before it drives out hatred. As you read these poems, let them remind you of the beauty in the world, feel them tap you into your feminine energy and inspire you to always lead with your heart.

Universal Purpose

What is your purpose?
What is your task?
To live, to love,
To show up for what the moment asks
Living is quite simple, you see
We are conscious agents here to Be
You want to change the world?
Then find what you love, and let it set
you free
This is the journey from duality
To oneness

Lucid Living

Life is but a dream
Where nothing is ever as it seems
It projects our internal reality
So we can heal our diseased mentalities
Oh, how we become focused on the tiny
things
When peace is never what this mindset
brings
Every enlightened being knows
That they create their day
They surrender to the flow
So the universe has space to bring
miracles their way

The Guide Inside

We run around all day
Thinking this is important
This we must do
But what can be more important
Than having a sacred appointment with you?
We ask everyone's opinion
Should I do this or that?
Go inside and ask yourself!
You'll never have to look back
Only you can give yourself clarity
So why do we trust ourselves so wearily?
As though another's seal of approval
Will save us from failures grasp
If we are always trying to avoid it
We will never succeed in any task
Trust the guide inside
The one whose voice is humble and wise
And if failure steps across your path
Do not try to avoid its wrath,
Instead ask what it is here to teach
Only through learning can your dreams be reached

Love Yourself Now

If you think all you are
Is who you could be
Then you will never experience
Your own divinity

Seeking Truth

We all seek a universal truth
It reveals itself through nature, animals,
and youth
Its song can only be heard when we
slow down
Through solitude and silence we'll finally
be found

Life plays this funny game
Where we seek truth through fortune,
lust, and fame
But truth has always lived within
Whispering wisdom to us in the ever-
changing winds

Truth touches us in glimpses of passion
We want to believe in magic yet bury it
in ration
Truth cannot be captured in words
And yet I still try, hoping I'm heard
We are blind to our own power
And enslaved to a matrix run by the
clock's hour
Like a rabbit chasing a carrot, we run in
circles,
Forgetting we are the Universe
Our consciousness eternal

If you are seeking a universal truth
Know that the Universe itself lives within
you
All the answers exist inside
Slow down, get still, open your eyes

Phoenix Rising

Problems arise when we forget who we
are
The consciousness behind our thoughts
The being made of dust from a billion-
year old star
But the path of love and creativity
Comes from finding your voice
From making even the simplest of
decisions a mindful choice
Always keep your shadow in front of you
Where you can see it
Make peace with the darkness in you
And you will find clarity beneath the
mind's mist
Like a phoenix rising you will be reborn
into the light
The strength of lessons learned laced
into your wings as you take flight

Celestial Harmony

Honor your phases
As you would the moon
You never look up and think
"You should be this or that,"
You honor her waning
How she faces darkness
And walks through her own shadow

You honor her waxing
How she grows and expands
Shining her light as bright as possible
You never think she should stay dark for
the Sun's comfort
You honor her fullness and allow her to
be wild

When she is waning again
She never fears that she will return to
the light
She honors all sides of herself equally
Knowing that there is a time for shadow
And there is a time for light
All things in nature embody this balance

Lens of Experience

We all see a virtual reality
Projected through individual mentalities
To a tree whose roots run deep
The universe is only knowable through
What its branches reach
To a bird that spreads her wings
She travels the world untethered
Seeing far off things

Some humans stay comfortable and
rooted
Afraid of the unknown, their minds
polluted
But for those of us who roam
The present moment is our eternal
home

There is a time to flap your wings
And a time when we must root to rise
Find this balance
And you will never feel lost inside

Time

A man-made law that binds us is Time
Everyone is under the illusion
That it works in a straight line

Past, present, and future exist all at
once
Déjà vu is merely an intuitive hunch
It is the ghost of a lesson we have
already learned
Reminding us to choose differently and
discern

Have you ever felt the day move too
fast?
Or feel time pass so slowly,
That it seems the moment will forever
last?
The clock marks how long we are alive
We think Time is killing us, but we do
not realize
We can speed Time up or slow it down
And let go of the idea that by a certain
age
We will be found,

Have fun in your twenties
And make a lot of money
Find that person
And settle in

Take medication to give yourself
A permanent grin
When will we wake up
And stop following what has been?

Where we are bound
Love will set us free
Untether your soul and don't let
Time, tell you who you should be
Play when you're eighty
And be wise at eighteen
Create your own reality
And never lose sight of your dreams

Patience

What is patience?
It is a spiritual form of waiting
I think I'd prefer to be immersed in the
now
Rather than wonder when
Things will manifest or how

Lessons from Trauma

I am the sum of all my ancestors who
came before
I have inherited their fear and anxiety
Wrapped up in traumas past worn
Not safe to have a voice, I lived silently

This was never mine to carry
It was never theirs
By facing these old traumas I receive
clarity
This ends with me and heals as I
become aware

When your pain body gets triggered
Remember "this isn't me."
As we let go of the belief that we're
internally injured
We'll come home to the pure part of us
that has always been free

Release Yourself Back to Yourself

Surrender your shame
You were once wild and untamed
This is your natural state of being
And it is where you shall return to
Remembering who you are is quite
freeing
And will heal all you have been through

Maintain your purity of heart
And your dancing soul
The world will try to change you
But You are more precious than any
gold

If everyone approves of you
Then it's time to give your life an
upheaval
Stand your ground empowered and true
Hold nothing back
And be unapologetically you

The Guru

Listen to your parents
Your friends
Your teachers
Honor their opinions
For they provide different perspectives

Leave the final say to the guru
The guru is the one that transforms
Dark into Light
It is the one who is honest and wise
Whose voice can only be heard
In silence and stillness
The guru is you

Intrinsic Worth

Slow down, breathe, my love
There will always be
Something important to attend to
And yet, what is more important than
To sit and be in total peace
We fear silence,
Yet through silence we are free
Prison only exists within
When we face our pain
We will no longer be held back by what
has been
Slow down, breathe, my love
Listen to the voice inside
It is wise, and wants you to be joyfully
alive
It intends that you actualize your soul's
potential
No longer living on autopilot
Or waiting for the world to hand you self-
worth
In a stack of credentials,
Your soul has intrinsic value
It has nothing to do with
With status, beauty, or success
Slow down, breathe, my love
Listen to the voice inside
You'll know what path to take
If you follow that inner guide

Meet Me in The Center

Give a gift to each person you meet
If you knew their whole story
You'd find none of your judgements to
be concrete
For in the end we are not so different

And all of us are equally significant
Our shells may vary in color and size
But we are connected through
Universal love inside

Give a gift to each person you meet
They have their own struggle beyond
what you see
Hate does not take a break
And fear spreads like wildfire
There is too much at stake
Lives are being sacrificed for dollars and
empires

Love must always be our response
The world cannot afford ignorance and
nonchalance
Everything that is happening directly
affects you,
Just because it is not at your doorstep
Does not make it of less value

We are each responsible for spreading
light
And leaving this world better
Ensuring everyone their rights

Good and evil do not exist
Pointing fingers only separates us from
bliss
I will meet you in the middle of Light and
Dark
Where we can stand in the center
United heart

From Lonely to Alone

At first becoming whole is lonely
We shed our old skin
And some relationships may temporarily
fade away
As the uncertainty of our identities are
shaken up
We become empty, but not in a hollow
way
In the way that space is empty and
contains the whole universe
We learn to belong to ourselves
And as our hearts become our home
We can learn to belong to the whole
world
To love it in its entirety
The fear of facing ourselves is when we
disconnect
And fall prey to illusions of separation
Unconditional love flows in when we are
brave enough
To face our own souls through eyes of
compassion
So it can then flow out and remind every
soul
That they are love itself

Untethered Love

People often come in and out of our
lives as messengers of light, as
wonderful teachers
Each of them carrying with them a
lesson
Some of them stay for a lifetime
Some of them only for a moment like a
bright comet passing by
But when we absorb the lesson we're
meant to learn from them
They continue along their way
We will always find what is meant for us
Whether we take this path or that
Different lessons all leading to the same
Truth
Love respects the free will of everyone's
journey
For it was never ours to command in the
first place

Purpose Beyond Perfection

I feel their eyes on me
All with their own opinions of how I
should be
There is always something I should
change
How do I keep my heart open?
I must stay focused in my lane

Stick to your vision
To what makes your heart soar
If you try to please everyone
You will never grow to be more

We don't need more perfect people
Sculpted by an idea that is unreachable
Be yourself and stay in your lane
If your work is true
It will see you through fear and pain

Let them see you how they please
They will praise you or judge you
Expectations impossible to meet
This was never between you and them

Follow your heart
And you will uncover the greatest gems
So many gifts hidden inside of you
The universe wants you to discover
them
To know you are courageous and true

And when you find them, give these gifts
to the world
Share with your whole heart
Whether they receive it as a rock or a
pearl

This has always been between you and
the universe
Maintain your integrity and you will be
immersed

In the greatest love you have ever
known
One that comes from inside
With an unshakeable purpose that
shows you
Why you are alive

Lessons From The Sea

Floating out in the turquoise sea
She wondered life's great mystery
Who are we, and how did we come to
be?

She gazed out observing the moonlit
tides
An undiscovered ocean with a world
underneath
The Sea gazed back, and wondered if
she'd realize
The answers are always hidden in plain
view
Simple and yet our doubt blinds us from
Truth

"I could tell her everything," the Sea
thought
But to be Awake- this can't be taught
Many wonder, but few are brave
To pass through life's trials, their hearts
untamed

Self-discovery is the key
To unlocking life's great mystery,
Dive underneath the chaotic waves
within
And you will discover Eternity
As it has always been

Stagnation

What do we do in times of stagnation?
Where we feel stuck and have lost
inspiration?

Sometimes, "it's all happening," seems
a false incantation
But remembering this truth is such a
simple salvation

We say go with the flow because life
comes in waves
There are times where our lives will
have too fast a pace

There are times when our to-do list will
overwhelm
And times when we will need to ask for
help

There are slow waves where we won't
know what to do
Where we forget our purpose and that
this is temporary too

We are gifted these times where not
much is happening
To learn the importance of connection
and tapping in

By slowing down and discovering we
are more
We can live each day more empowered
than before

Then return to the fast pace of life with
fresh eyes
Tapped into a deeper layer of love
inside

Dissolving Barriers

Who do you think you are?
It is strange how we confuse
Self-deprecation with being humble
The voice in our head loves to abuse
And bury truth beneath its harsh jumble

How do you speak about yourself?
Do you feel proud or rejoice in your
inner wealth?
Do you walk down the street confident
and free?
Or have you forgotten this is how we are
naturally meant to be?

Never be afraid to shine your light
Expand and take up more space than
you think is right
Recall the Wild Soul within
And know your spirit expands
Beyond your skin

Lessons from Anger

Anger is the energy of transformation
It is a volcano erupting and giving birth
to an island
Use it as a catalyst for honest
contemplation
If you speak to it in the safety of silence
It will reveal what is important to you
And what you hold yourself back from
Allow the full expression of anger to
come through
And harness its energy to empower the
beat of your own drum
Transform it to fuel your creative fire
Let it become the unstoppable force that
manifests your desires

Art Awakens the Heart

Let your art be the tether
That brings you home to your heart
If you start to view life
Through a magnifying glass
Practice an art and you will see
None of your worries last

Art is alchemy, free and bold
It can turn the heaviest situation of lead
Into the wisest lesson of gold
It helps us to understand why
Through all challenges and changes of
life

Art is the language of the universe
It speaks to us in drops of paint
Or in the ink of a writer's pen
It burns through any constraint
The flame of creativity is alive in us all
It is medicine for the soul
And can break down any wall

Art can take the shape of any mold
It is fluid, ever-changing
Art cannot be pinned into a hole,
Look for Art's presence everywhere and
you will see
It is throughout all of nature
And the very lungs you breathe

Origins

Creativity is the pulse of our intuition
It burns through the limitations of the
mind
So our dreams can come into fruition
Pleasure is how we control time
And through this immersion of presence
Our mind, body, and spirit aligns
To the origins of our infinite essence

Patient Pursuit

Perhaps the answer is never "no,"
But rather, "not now"
What we think we want
Is based on what we know

But perhaps what we do not know
Is that there is something much better
Already on its way
When you wish and manifest
Or when you pray
Make sure to add,
"This or something better,"
Instead of getting stuck on what you
crave

Be content with what is
The more gratitude you feel
The more you will attract bliss

Always be excited for what is to come
For our dreaming is never truly done
Know you are never lacking
For all things are one

Hold Nothing Back

We receive in life
What we are bold enough
To take action with
But rejection haunts us
And prevents us
From feeling empowered by this

We have a short amount of time
On this spinning blue ball
So leap regardless of
If the net appears
You are not on this planet to crawl

Expectations

We all see through the lens of our
personal experience
No two realities the same
Too many different expectations
Impossible to maintain

How can I balance everyone's
happiness,
While maintaining the integrity of my
heart?
I must hold strong boundaries
And see each being as a work of art

Some will trigger you, frustrate you, or
upset you
But you are responsible for
remembering the truth
That Spirit lives within them too
And if we are to let go of reaction
Then we must surrender the resentment
behind every action
The solution is to see through the eyes
of love

For no character defect is fatal
And every alchemist is infinitely able,
To mend the deepest wounds
And support every flower on their
journey to bloom
The Medicine of an Open Heart

Strength is keeping our hearts open
Instead of becoming hardened by life's
trials
Insecurity will always be loud and
demanding
It needs to be seen and validated
constantly
Compassion is subtle
Compassion is our truest form of
strength
Our power lies in empathy
Empathy provides understanding
And understanding alleviates suffering

The Lesson of Arrows

Human beings are always shooting out
imaginary arrows
That are meant to be intercepted by
someone else
Depending on what we are meant to
learn at that time

And when two people's arrows intercept
There is a moment that changes a
person's life
Into what it is meant to be

Our arrows never miss their target
People walk into our lives with purpose
Shining light on what we need to heal
Within ourselves

Blank Slate

I challenge you
Hit the reset button
Go a day where you let go of any ideas
About who you think you are
Who anyone else is
And what you have learned about life
thus far

Walk through a day with a blank slate
Allow the world to show you a new side
of itself
Let your certainty be shaken up and
cracked open
You cannot become all that you are
meant to be
By staying where you are

Waking up From Our Amnesia

What do we do when hope is gone?
When the light is out, and we are
floating along?
How do we ignite the flame within?
We are a species with amnesia
Holding on to what has been
Killing nature for instant gratification
Trading our Mother for a virtual reality to
escape in
The further away we get from truth
Chasing validation and eternal youth
Numbing ourselves in every way
Television, drugs, and phones over play

We present ourselves as a flawless
mirage
Where few can see through our layered
façade
How do we ignite the flame within?
By remembering we are the gods we
have always been
When one of us is hurt, all of us bleed
We must equally honor the spirit of
every flower and weed,
We are souls passing through a
parenthesis of infinity

To heal the world
We must honor its divinity
Change starts with you
Heal yourself, wake up, and know this to
be true
The wisdom of the cosmos dwell within
you

Nature's Womb

The womb is the portal life comes
through
She moves through the birth and death
of nature
In harmony with the cycles of the moon
She carries within her the wisdom of the
earth
Within this masculine paradigm we have
forgotten her worth
When I speak to her and ask, "where
does it hurt?"
I feel her pain spread through every sea,
city, and desert

Conflict Creates Miracles

Do not avoid conflict
Conflict is merely energy colliding
It is nature's special way of guiding
Just like every canyon or beautiful
beach
All miracles are born out of chaos
The contrast is what releases them free
There is no dream that is out of reach
This is how all things came to be
A seed never questions it will grow
Into the mightiest tree

The Way

By being tethered to past trauma
We are held captive by the mind's
drama
As we remain in the present moment
We relax and our lives continue flowing
Our breath is the password to enter
peace
Through silence and stillness
We can witness our old patterns release
By shattering the mind's illusions, what
is there to gain?
We are human beings after all
Enlightenment won't protect us from
pain
By remembering who we are
We stop seeking for a way and become
The Way

The Mystery of Simplicity

You can search for the answers in every
land
Or you can see the earth's history in a
grain of sand
The map of our ancestors laid out in the
palm of your hand
Life will reveal its secrets when we
surrender instead of demand

Empowerment Within, Freedom Without

What we fear outside
Already exists within
When we heal inside
Our external fears will lose their power

Communication

Words do not just disappear into the
void
Their vibrations circle the earth
They can either heal or destroy
"Be impeccable with your word,"
This is a challenging thing to ask
When many people fear unfiltered
honesty
And instead hide behind a sugary mask

The secret of communication
Is not in the power of words
It lays in our ability to make people feel
heard
Listen with your heart
You will truly understand
You will see into their soul
And know the power of a helping hand

The River

There is a river with your name on it
With a strong current that moves
In fluidity and grace
Surrender and flow with the river of your
life

If you battle upstream
You will only resist the miracles
That are on their way to you
You can never step in the same river
twice
You will never again live the same
moment of life

When nothing feels right
Get back into the river with your name
on it
And appreciate each moment for what it
is
Your job is to allow it to carry you
Without fear or resistance

Trials and challenges do not come
Because life is against you
They are wonderful teachers,
That sculpt our souls
They mirror to us our strength
And when we no longer fight or play
victim
The dam in our mind's is removed
And the river can carry us to the next
level
Until we remember we are whole

This Too Shall Pass

In the depths of depression
My mother said to me,
"This too shall pass,"
For all things are temporary
And nothing truly lasts

In my highest state of ecstasy
When I was untethered and wild
My mother gave me her wisest, knowing
smile
She saw into the depths of me and said,
"This too shall pass,"
For all things shift and change
And this moment shall never be the
same

Self-Care is Love

How do I balance a generous heart
With the balance of self-care
Where do I start?
If we are not all equal in life's game
Then how do I remember we are all the
same?
Can you treat a struggling stranger
With the same kindness as your loved
one?
To burn out being of service is
disingenuous
It is now that I realize self-care is truly
generous
This is how we give without expectation
To stand unwavering in the strength of
our own love
And emit healing vibrations
We must create healthy boundaries
Be prepared for the universe will test
them profoundly
We cannot give what we do not have
Always balance the mind, body, soul
triad
Through this unity we can heal what is
broken
For when we open our eyes and see
only love
Our eyes will truly be open

The Lightheartedness of Being

Sweet soul
Do not worry so much
Your life energy is precious
Do not waste it trying to figure things out
Your victory is already assured

Knowing the future would simply
Pull you from the present
You are right where you are meant to be
All other moments have lead you to this
door
And prepared you for this moment
May the highest version of your soul
That is ready to integrate
Live through you now
It is time, it is time

The Universe Inside

I look into your eyes
And I do not see a color
I see the entire cosmos
Reflected back to me

I see eternity in the recycled atoms
That make up the work of art
That is you

Love Beyond Illusions

Falling in love
Is a temporary vacation
From the mind's suffering

But to truly awaken
We must fall in love
With ourselves unconditionally
Before we can extend this
To another soul
Conditional love
Only tries to control
But unconditional love
Is to create value and happiness
For yourself
And remain whole

Regardless of if the other stays
This value and happiness
Cannot be taken away
True love is transcendent of labels and
games
It is a way for the universe
To experience itself
In the most powerful way

Love's Mirror

You want someone to look
Into your soul
And love all that you are
Do you look into your soul
And love all that you are?

You want someone to fully accept
Support and care for you
Do you fully accept, support,
And care for yourself?

True love begins intrinsically
Only then can two independent flames
Come together and ignite a wildfire

Lessons from a Tree

I would like to be a tree
Whose roots run deep
Whose branches grow tall
Those who gaze at her
Become present and enthralled

On the surface, she is beautiful
But her service to life
Is indisputable
She provides shade and a home
For all the creatures who roam

With her unconditional love
She transforms toxins
Into oxygen
From the sunlight above

Even as we cut her down
She is forgiving
For she knows
The impermanence of living
And allows her formless energy
To be recycled
As nature works in synergy

Warriors of Light

Before walking onto the battlefield
Paint a butterfly upon your shield
This is what it means to be a Warrior of
Light
To shoot Loves arrow in every fight

Love is the water that cools hate's flame
Compassion is our reminder that we are
all the same
Now is not the time to idly sit by
While freedom is stripped away and
innocents die

Every single one of us makes a
difference
Whether we realize it or not
We can no longer fall prey to ignorance

Moment to moment we have a choice
To numb, disconnect, or use our voice
Speak your truth and speak it loud
One strong voice can change
The mind of any crowd,

The earth's bleeding heart can seem,
Impossible to heal
Just start at the place that feels most
real

Pick a cause that feels genuine to you
And do your best to see it through
Do not be of service out of obligation
But instead show up out of love,
respect, and
To raise the vibration

The Law of Attraction

Thoughts do not just disappear
They emit vibrations
Into the atmosphere

Your voice is your most powerful tool
In creating a reality set by your own
rules
Speak up with what works for you
Your dreams will be successful
If you honor what is true

To apply the law of attraction
Be mindful of your intention behind
every action
Speak your life into being
As though it has already happened

First tap into your inner mystery
Visualize your dream life
As though it is already a memory
The universe responds to belief,

The world will change
As you take bigger leaps
Life alters through your lens of
perception
Know your worth
And practice reception

Traveling to Myself

The more places I go
The more I realize I will never
Fully understand this world
Through the eyes of logic
But when I close my eyes
And find stillness in my heart
I can feel it
It's a part of me
It's a part of you

Facing Your Soul

When we skip over our pain
And go straight to positivity
It is like floating on the surface of the
ocean
Looking for a treasure that only exists in
the depths
You cannot reach dawn without walking
through the night
A seed is planted in darkness before it
grows towards the light

The Golden Key

Anytime another triggers you
Or hurts you
Anytime you judge another
A golden key is being revealed to you

This pain is a blessing
For it is revealing the part of you that is
unhealed
So you can face your own soul
And release all that holds you back

You are not a victim of circumstance
You have called this in
Because you are ready to be more than
what you have been

The Whole is unconditional love and
acceptance
Just look at any deity, master, or leader
They used every situation as a catalyst
for healing

In bringing forth even more light
Be awake to all challenges
And recognize them as a golden key
Look inside yourself

Why does this hurt?
Where does this come from?
How can we forgive ourselves and let
go?

See passed the mistake of another and
into the divine in them
So you can see past the pain inside you
and know the divine as yourself

Merging in the Now

Time moves within and without us
Through endless spirals
With all things merging as one
In the here and now
See eternity through
The twinkling cosmic ocean
Or hold infinity in a small seed
Whichever lens you look through
It will all lead you back to this moment

Ubuntu

Underneath it all
We crave the same thing
Love, connection, belonging
To see and be seen
To feel and be felt
If we stripped down
To the deepest motivation behind every
action
We would see into our hearts desires
And recognize the thread that connects
every soul
The infinite energy that lives and
breathes through us
Is the very Love we are searching for

The Eye of the Cosmic Storm

Transcendence is achieved through the
eyes of love
When we stop waiting around for a sign
from above
Fate is not in charge you see
We cannot always rest on the excuse
that all things are meant to be
Though certain things are written, our
hearts are always free
Every moment we have the choice of
what direction to go in
Free Will has no compass

And if your spirit does not stop at the
barrier of your skin
Then what are the limits to where we
can go?
That my love, only you will know
As you take down the barriers you have
built within your mind
As you break the bondage of societal
agreements and the laws of time

You can get to wherever you want to be
from wherever you are,
Once you remember that there was
never a set bar
You are ancient atoms recycled and
transformed
The secret to happiness is learning to
dance in the eye of every storm

So Hum – I am that I am

The moment we identify what Love is
We merely identify what it is not
If you are a seeker of Love
Do not seek the edges of the earth
Seek within
You can travel to the edges of your soul
Only to find there are none
For you are the is-ness that merges with
everything

Inner Animal

A leaf came down and kissed me on the
face
As I looked up I saw a bird take flight
Its wings spread beneath the sun's rays

We spend so much of our lives looking
down
Getting lost in the chatter of our mind's
Or stressfully running around

As the bird flew away
I felt the warm sun kiss my skin
And imagined my own wings spreading
For in our deepest state we are akin

This bird symbolized freedom from
desire
Call on the animal of your choice
Whose qualities you most admire
Get outside of yourself and away from
the mind's voice
Slip into your animal skin
For in your untamed wildness
You'll find autonomy within

Spiritual Paralysis

Knowing too much becomes spiritual
paralysis
Unable to jump first and ask questions
later
Experience has been squandered by
over-analysis
I can map out the entire ocean for you
And tell you all its coordinates and facts
But I have yet to swim underneath the
big blue
And feel a wave's impact
Knowledge crumbles on the hard shell
of the mind
Until it is lived as experience in the heart
Then it can become wisdom beyond
time
There are no mistakes if we learn
They become colorful stories that make
up our being
Though it is important to always discern,
Life is made up of courageous moments
Where we dissolve our limits
And find deeper meaning

What Does Your Life Reflect?

And I hope your choices reflect
Your dreams and not your fears
For we are the size of tiny insects
In the many galaxies of the cosmos

Do not waste your one life playing small
Feel the full range of who you are
Every moment you live
Bring the light and fire of the brightest
star

And always make sure to forgive
You are meant for more than
Holding on to old scars
The most beautiful creations were born
in darkness

Joined with the light of perspective and
experience
Always keep creating regardless
And stay passionately curious
Wisdom is failure alchemized

Passed down to those brave enough
To take new strides
As Dark and Light intersect,
I hope boldness and bravery
Are what your life reflects

Contradictions

As living beings, we are always evolving
Our DNA itself grows and changes
We create problems to feel good about
solving
And have forgotten the wisdom of the
ages

This is not the age of wisdom
It is the age of information
All certainty of our belief systems
Have been cracked open and shaken

"There is one Truth," they say
Though no one seems to know what it is
Religion, science, and spirituality are all
the "right" way
Though each other they dismiss

Perhaps I contradict my beliefs
They are always shifting
And to me this is a relief
For to believe one thing my entire life
Is to ensure that from Truth I'll be
drifting,

I do not trust those that stay the same
It means they are submissive
To society's complex game
It means to their heart they are
dismissive
And choose security over growth

Question everything
Especially you
And to one idea, never cling
This way you will discern what's true
To believe strongly
Limits our perception of the world
There are infinite possibilities
Beyond what the human brain
Can perceive

Beyond the Surface

Why do we always ask the same
questions?
What is your name?
Where are you from?
What do you do?

This teaches us nothing about what they
have been through
We learn little about who they truly are
Their hopes and dreams or how they
learned from their scars

There is a mechanicalness in the
average conversation
We are either on autopilot or caught in
our agendas fixation
Sometimes we ask new questions out of
infatuation

We must ask better questions for the
sake of connection
Stories unite us and dissolve our fear of
rejection
Each being is a teacher and can give
you a gift,
A lesson that will bring you closer to
finding your bliss

Our deepest connections often come in
The form of who we least expect
They smack us awake
And show us what we need to accept

Unconditional love is the end game
It is how we heal conditioning and deep
rooted shame
So, what questions can we ask
To see through each other's mask?
Expansive questions have the power to
unlock any door
They will help us find deeper connection
than before

Intertwined Yet Free

There's no place I'd rather be
Than down by the sparkling sea
It is here I dream of you and me
Our hearts intertwined, yet free

Courage is all Love asks
She prays we are up to the task
In True Love we must take off our
masks
The Source of our souls reflected back

When you see into someone's heart
And know their spirit to be pure
Recognize the universe in them
Beyond the naked eyes allure

Questions For The Cosmos

When the big bang occurred
Did time and space emerge with it?
The answers seem to be a blur
Buried beneath too many opinions

How are colors made in the universe?
Beyond refractions of light
And are we in a multiverse?
With dimensions and portals alike?

How is love made in scientific terms?
Or is it unexplained, immeasurable
poetry?
Is experience the only way in which we
can truly learn?
And what does it mean to be a soul
that's free?

Can the power of the mind,
Heal illness and transcend time?
And what are we doing here in the first
place?
Is it all random and pointless, a trial of
free will?

Or is it governed by destiny and fate?
I pray to these mysteries the universe
will one day spill

Until then I shall live the questions
For I think exploring them
Is our greatest creative expression

We're human beings, after all
Both one with the universe
And yet incredibly small
We all seem to be making this up as we
go

So enjoy life like a huge party
But don't forget to grow
Balance is the center of contrast
To live numbly or in ecstasy is a choice
For even the world itself won't last

Eternal Beings

Eternity slumbers in me
And She will only awaken
When I open my heart
To where She already resides
And allow her to merge with infinity

The Intersection of Life

Our stories are precious gifts
Laced with lessons
Embodying the paradox of being
Share your story with your heart and
soul
It is a message for all those who listen
We did not come to know each other by
accident
This sharing of time and space
When we entrust each other with our
stories
A cosmic energy spirals throughout us

The Awakening

When I found home within myself
I was free
When I truly loved myself
I opened my eyes
And could finally see
I gazed at everything
And recognized it as me

Melt into Me

As we leave our mind's astray
Our spirits grow beyond the milky way
I have never known a heart so pure
I recognize those ancient eyes
Deeper than your shells allure
A cosmic ocean flowing inside
Energetic waves of consciousness
As you teach me to surf
My life's journey with confidence
The fears of my mind can no longer
prevail
For I now see all that is not love
As an illusory tale
Our love is a flame that never burns
It merely ignites our purpose
Deepening our ability to learn

Moving Meditation

Movement is the language of feeling
Through the exploration of my body and
breath
I am learning the art of being
And if the path appears everywhere that
we step
Then there are no wrong turns
And we become free of regrets
Choice is merely an act of hesitation
Where we imagine all outcomes
And get lost in stagnation
Each moment shapes who we become
But our decisions are impermanent
since
All things are One
Trust all is happening, and never stress
over how
The only moment you'll ever arrive to is
Now

Certainty vs. Mystery

The only thing that can be known
Is the unknown
Fall in love with the mystery
The universal soul cannot be
Understood through ration
It is felt in its entirety
Through the silence and stillness of
Being

Freedom of Possession

Love is an infinite dance with the
universe
It is a fire igniting in unspoken words
Setting aflame the dark corners within
us we had thought forgotten
Love's fire can only exist where there is
oxygen
Possession extinguishes this fire, and if
love is the oxygen of life
Then we respect the will of all beings
that cross our path

Awakened Wanderlust

Oh, to dream of far off places
Cobblestone streets and different
cultural paces
The aroma of espresso, pastries and
crisp air
The sounds of celebration, movement,
life
New explorations shared
Reading an old book at a little café
Writing about the characters
That walk by throughout the day
This is the traveler's way
To roam through time and space
Our perspectives constantly shifting
states

Garden of Eden

Can you be present,
And use your imagination at the same
time?
Time itself is merely a construct of the
mind
And if the imagination is the bridge
To our intuition
Then we must set ourselves free
And stop waiting for anyone else's
permission
Anxiety is a waste of the imagination
Meant to keep us suffering
Follow the pull of your heart
It is your passport to freedom
Paradise dwells within
And reveals itself only when
We stop seeking an external Garden of
Eden

Arrive

We have nowhere to go
Nowhere to arrive
This is an illusion
Distracting us from
The eternal wealth inside

Lessons from Pain

Crack my heart open so new light can
come in
As I learn to dance with my shadow
I return to the spark of divinity I have
always been
You have been my mirror and torn down
my walls
I will never run from Love's pain
For if I am to become Love itself
I will embrace it entirely and never play
games
I am formless form
Expanding beyond this shell
My heart and soul no longer torn
As I become free of my mind's hell

Lessons from Power

What is power?
The life force of the present that arises
from within
It is the energy of love
That is beyond the sum of who we have
been
What is awakening?
To still exist within time and space
But to be grounded in the truth of the
present
Free of the mind's race
What is service?
Mirroring the goodness of every soul
So they too can know love's power and
merge in with the whole

Lessons from a Spider

I have roots that roam
Like a spider weaving her web
I create an infinite amount of homes
Never attached to one place I go
I surrender to the direction
The river of spirit flows

I string my own fate
On an iridescent silk thread
It is strong yet subject to change
When my masterpiece is destroyed
I do not feel dread
All things return to an infinite void
I create simply for my spirits joy

Thought Loops

How do I still my brains chatter
And silence any thought loops
That reinforce old patterns
The answer is not about silencing the
voice at all
It can be of deep service
But it can also create walls
So I shall tell you of its purpose
But do not give it more power than this
For the voice can also create suffering
Or it can be the foundation of bliss

The brain uses itself to understand its
own existence
A miracle forgotten so easily
When we believe its illusions we create
resistance
The magic of the Now overlooked
ceaselessly

We are the only animals on this planet
That can decide what life to live
This too, we take for granted
But the present moment always forgives

Cosmic Humor

How do I have an open heart?
In a world of such suffering
Where do I start?

In an age of skepticism and digital
isolation
The antidote is creative activism
And spiritual transformation

Keep your heart open
And do not worry about rejection
For everything is a mere projection
The key to empowerment is self-
acceptance

And if it's true that this is all a dream
Then our beliefs should never be taken
to the extreme
A cosmic sense of humor will help us
see
That our only universal purpose is to
learn how to Be

The Future

What if we stopped asking,
"How will this turn out?"
And ceased wondering
If we're meant to take a certain route

What if we recognized
Our path is wherever we step?
And released feeling lost
Or caught in a wave of regret

What if we no longer
Held on to what has been?
And remembered we are
Weavers of our fate
Creating a web of magic within

Masters of Fate

We are Queens and Kings
All dressed in rags
Too focused on small things
Forgetting the power we once had

Roll your shoulders back
Feel the universe you hold in your heart
Get back on your soul's path
Remember the royal you've been from
the start

To be a master of your fate
Holds great responsibility
We must use it in a loving way
Empowering others to find peace

Do you remember what it was like?
When your body worked in harmony
with nature
When you were tuned in to all of life?
For as we become one, our power is
greater

La Luna

She lights the way
And invites you into the dark
Her iridescence cannot be seen by day
At night she's a ruler of the stars
She controls the tides of psychic flow
And teaches us to love our darkness
So we may fully embody our inner glow
She is the seer of souls
From her eye's we cannot hide
If you seek to learn from her mystery
Be prepared to grow
And live from a deeper layer of love
inside

Kali

You may know me as the destroyer
I shatter ignorance and illusion
To allow your true self to come forward
My purifying anger incinerates the minds
confusion

I am shadow wrapped in stars
I translate the wisdom of the moon
You will find me in the lessons of your
scars
Though the ego I consume

I am the energy of chaos
To the brave I birth new life
Those who value comfort are forever
lost
I am unapologetic in my
transformational tides

What We are Made of

I am of the earth
My heart is the deepest part of the sea
The flowers are my lips
My eyes exist within every tree
The curve of their branches my hips
My arms are the wings of every bird
My spine forged by mountains
Through the wind you'll hear my
whispering word
My energy is always surrounding
I am the rays of the sun that warm your
skin
Helping you to meet your truth within
You are of the earth
Sink into your body's wisdom
And you shall know your worth
Beyond the bondage of time or distance

Faith over Fear

Watch when your certainty is shaken
How many thoughts will flood your mind
Like fear in the form of horses racing
The illusion of control shattered in time

It is much easier to stay in the comfort of
what we know
But evolution is a trust fall
And the unknown is how we grow

We are the entire universe experiencing
itself in this form
Uncertainty is when our existence is
most honest
As we bring deeper awareness to the
life we explore
There is no such thing as a permanent
promise
For we are only guaranteed the now
Every supernova is unpredictable yet
flawless
It is in our nature to transform
And we never truly decide when or how

Conscious Connection

Look into a person's eyes
And be present for their soul
This is more healing
Than you could ever know
I honor the place in you
Where the entire universe resides
This conscious connection is why we
are alive

Respect the Roses Thorns

I am the red rose whose stem you tried
to pull
And contain in a small vase of your fear
Instead my roots grew deeper and my
thorns full
For all that you are has become clear
I am the ocean you tried to contain in a
drop
But my tides have only grown more wild
I have met the truth inside myself and
can no longer be stopped
Through your lessons my heart and I
have reconciled

Belonging

When you belong to yourself
You belong to the world
You can access the wisdom of every
cell
If you're first willing to be unnerved
We often ask why the ground beneath
us is being shaken
Not realizing that surrendered
uncertainty
Is what guides us to awaken

It is time

Women, it is time
Nothing is more unstoppable
Then when a Goddess decides to rise
Her magic is the kind that makes
moving mountains possible

Men, it is time
For you to know your true power
Not what you have felt in this paradigm
But instead what it is to live vulnerably
By crumbling the protective walls you
built in your hearts tower

We are so much more than our minds
can comprehend
The synergy of masculine and feminine
Reveals our oneness as it has always
been
Through this truth the duality of human
nature can begin to transcend

Acknowledgements

I would like to thank the following people for their inspiration and encouragement...

Raquelle Mantra, my soul sister who actively listened to every poem as I wrote them. You are the most genuine, compassionate person I have met and my magic partner in crime.

My mother, who is a living example of courage and unapologetically herself. She truly understands the art of deep listening. I wouldn't be on this strange, wonderful journey called life without you mama.

Alexis, my sister, there are no words for what you are to me. Thank you for always helping me find the joy and humor in every situation. Your cosmic soul is essential.

My dad, who has the smartest brain I know and taught me what passionate curiosity is.

Alexandra Gallagher, you were the first one to read this the whole way through. Thank you for exploring the whole world with me.

Wendy Both, thank you for helping me begin this journey. You are a wonderful healer and have always encouraged me to follow my heart's path.

Deanna Ainsworth, thank you for believing in the 18-year-old girl that walked into your yoga studio trying to find herself. You are one of the most selfless people I have ever met.

Angelica Singh, without your craniosacral training I never would have learned to face my shadow. Thank you for helping people become embodied.

Dr. Keshava, whose meditation training altered the course of my path. Thank you for teaching me that meditation is not an action, but a quality of awareness to bring to every action.

The star tribe in Hawaii, these poems are largely inspired by you and what I learned from your love.

Jade Alectra, you are a true master. Thank you for igniting a fire in all of our hearts.

Dean and the Venice Tribe, the love you guys embody is changing the world.

Alyssa Foggiatto, you are so much more than an agent and believed in what I was doing before I did. Thank you.

Jill Wintersteen, you are a goddess. An alchemist. Your vulnerability inspires me, and having your energy in this book is an honor.

Rebecca Reitz, you brought the formless into form with this cover. The way you combine your intuition with your art is unique and very needed in this world. Thank you for everything.

To every cosmic soul that has crossed my path whether virtually or in person, The Your Own Magic tribe, I see you. I believe in you. I love you. There are no words to express the honor it is to be a part of this existence with you.

Made in the USA
San Bernardino, CA
31 January 2018